METAMORPHIC ROCKS

by Ava Sawyer

CAPSTONE PRESS
a capstone imprint

Fact Finders Books are published by Capstone Press,
1710 Roe Crest Drive, North Mankato, Minnesota 56003
www.mycapstone.com

Library of Congress Cataloging-in-Publication Data
Names: Sawyer, Ava, author.
Title: Metamorphic rocks / by Ava Sawyer.
Description: North Mankato, Minnesota : Capstone Press, [2018] |
    Series: Fact finders. Rocks | Audience: Ages 8–10. | Includes index.
Identifiers: LCCN 2017059334 (print) | LCCN 2018005719 (ebook)
    | ISBN 9781543527186 (ebook PDF) | ISBN 9781543527025
    (library binding) | ISBN 9781543527100 (paperback)
Subjects: LCSH: Metamorphic rocks—Juvenile literature. |
    Petrology—Juvenile literature.
Classification: LCC QE475.A2 (ebook) | LCC QE475.A2 S385 2018
    (print) | DDC 552/.4—dc23
LC record available at https://lccn.loc.gov/2017059334

Editorial Credits
Editor: Nikki Potts
Designer: Sarah Bennett
Media Reseacher: Jo Miller
Production Specialist: Laura Manthe

Image Credits
Science Source: B. Murton/Southampton Oceanography Centre,
25, Gary Hincks, 17 (bottom); Shutterstock: alybaba, 22, Amit
kg, 5, Anton Foltin, 2, 17 (top), Artesia Wells, 26, Barnes Ian, 12,
BlackRabbit3, 11, Designua, 23, Federico Rostagno, 8, hapelena,
7 (top), Landscape Nature Photo, 20, Laszio Szirtesi, 9, luca85, 7
(top middle), Marty Nelson, 24, milart, 21, minik, 28, Nickola_Che,
6, 19 (bottom), Nikitin Victor, cover, Petr Bonek, 29 (left), Roy
Palmer, 7 (bottom), Stella Photography, 29 (right), Ted PAGEL, 18,
Tom Grundy, 14, Tyler Boyes, 19 (top), Vitoriano Junior, 14, vvoe,
7 (bottom middle)

Design Elements
Shutterstock: Alted Studio, Chris Warham

Printed in the United States of America.
PA021

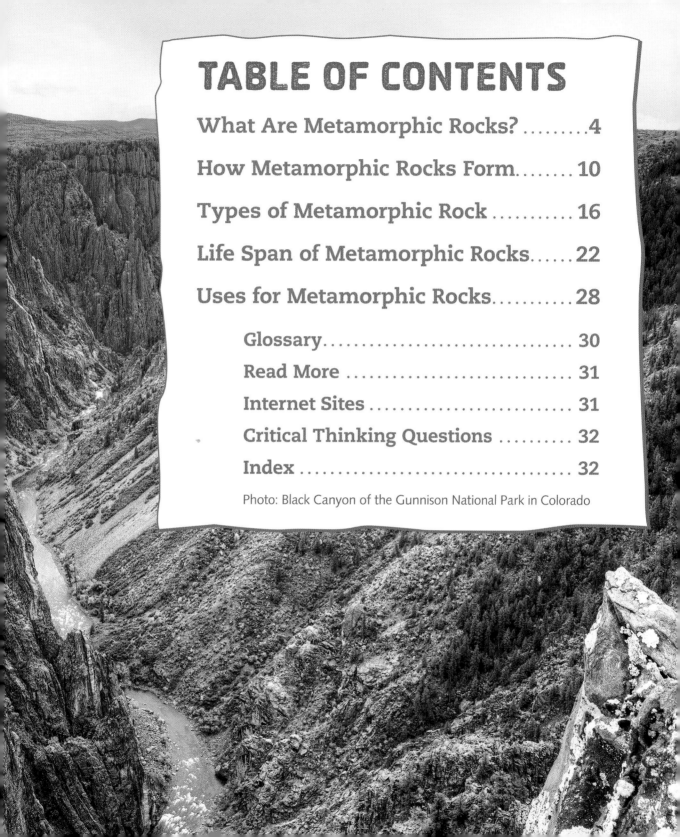

TABLE OF CONTENTS

Photo: Black Canyon of the Gunnison National Park in Colorado

CHAPTER 1

WHAT ARE METAMORPHIC ROCKS?

Between the mild conditions at Earth's surface and the tremendous temperatures and pressures within Earth, rocks undergo many changes. There are three types of rock—metamorphic, igneous, and sedimentary. Rocks that have changed from one type of rock to another are metamorphic rocks. Some metamorphic rocks used to be igneous rock. Some used to be sedimentary rock. Other metamorphic rocks used to be a different type of metamorphic rock.

The word *metamorphic* comes from Greek words that mean "to change form." This word may be familiar because it also applies to animals that change from one form to another. For example, frogs change from tadpoles to adult frogs. The animal in the early stage looks nothing like the adult animal.

The same thing happens with rocks that go through the process of metamorphosis. When a rock is placed under intense heat or pressure, changes occur. A new rock is formed. The new rock looks and feels completely different than the old rock. Any rock that has tremendous heat or pressure applied to it can turn into a different type of rock.

Metamorphic rock makes up part of the Himalayas in India.

Metamorphic rocks are made from materials called minerals. Some metamorphic rocks are made out of just one mineral. Others are made up of many types of minerals. The minerals inside rocks are made up of atoms that are arranged in rows and columns that form **crystals**. All metamorphic rocks include some type of crystals.

Nothing is added to the rocks as they go through the process of metamorphism. Nothing is taken away either. However, the minerals that make up the rocks are changed during the process. When the minerals change, so does the rock they make up.

During this process, the original minerals break down and the crystals of new minerals form. For example, metamorphic rocks heat up and begin to reach the **melting point** as they move through the rock cycle. More and more of the minerals in the metamorphic rock begin to change into those found in igneous rock. These minerals include quartz, feldspar, and biotite.

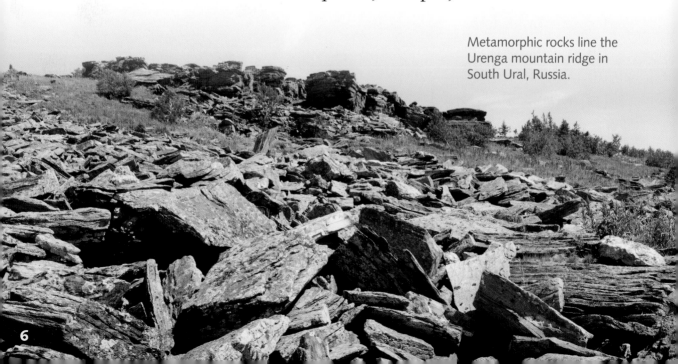

Metamorphic rocks line the Urenga mountain ridge in South Ural, Russia.

MINERALS

All rocks are made up of minerals. Minerals are natural, nonliving, solid materials. Each mineral is made of one or more elements. An element is a substance that contains only one kind of atom. Geologists have found about 3,000 minerals on Earth. However, most of them are rare. Only around 100 of them are commonly found in rocks.

Many of the minerals found in metamorphic rocks are not found in other rocks. Chlorite, for example, is found only in the metamorphic rocks slate and phyllite. Garnet, staurolite, and kyanite are also minerals only found in metamorphic rocks.

chlorite

garnet

staurolite

kyanite

....
crystal—a solid substance having a regular pattern of many flat surfaces

melting point—the temperature when a solid turns into a liquid when heated

geologist—someone who studies minerals, rocks, and soil

Metamorphic rocks are usually hard. They are dull in appearance, meaning they are not shiny. They are also fairly rough to the touch. If a person wants to use marble—for a sculpture, for example—it only becomes smooth during the carving and polishing process.

Carrara marble quarries in Tuscany, Italy

PIETÁ

In 1498, a young Italian artist named Michelangelo was hired by a Roman Catholic cardinal to create a religious sculpture. The sculpture was to be a life-sized *Pietá*—a representation of Jesus being cradled by his mother after his crucifixion.

Michelangelo selected a large block of marble from the rock quarries around the city of Carrara in northern Italy. The slab of marble was 6 feet (2 meters) long and 5 feet (1.5 m) high.

Michelangelo worked for two years hammering, drilling, and polishing the block of metamorphic rock. His *Pietá* became one of the most famous sculptures in the world. Today the *Pietá* is on display at St. Peter's Basilica at the Vatican in Rome.

Michelangelo became one of the greatest artists of all time. He continued to create sculptures and often chose marble as his medium.

Michelangelo's completed *Pietá*

CHAPTER 2

HOW METAMORPHIC ROCKS FORM

Earth has three main parts. At the center is the core. Around the core is the mantle, which is a very hot place where solid rock turns to molten rock. Around the mantle is the crust, which forms Earth's outer surface.

The crust is made up of tectonic plates. When molten rock from the mantle called magma rises through the crust, it becomes lava. Not all magma comes from the mantle, though. In some places, material in the crust melts and forms magma chambers close to Earth's surface.

Metamorphic rocks are formed when extreme heat, pressure, or a combination of the two is applied to rocks. Local metamorphism, also called contact metamorphism, requires magma. Magma can get hotter than 1,832 degrees Fahrenheit (1,000 degrees Celsius). Rocks that are closest to the magma—especially those that are in contact with it—are affected the most. Those rocks become the hottest and change the most during metamorphism. Rocks that are farther from the magma's heat change less in the process. Rocks that are far enough away from the magma so that its heat does not reach them are not affected. Those rocks remain unchanged.

Susa Hornfels in Hagi, Japan

One example of local metamorphism is when magma flows next to mudstone. The heat from the magma causes the mineral crystals in the mudstone to form new patterns. The result is a new metamorphic rock called hornfels.

tectonic plate—a gigantic slab of Earth's crust that moves around on magma

hornfels—a metamorphic rock formed by the contact between mudstone or shale and a hot igneous body

Rocks are placed under pressure in a couple of ways. First, imagine if a person was covered by every blanket, coat, and piece of clothing in the house. One blanket or coat might not be too heavy. However, each new layer would add more and more weight on top of the person's body. The same is true with Earth. Earth's crust is made up of layers of rocks. The rocks on the bottom feel intense pressure as more and more rocks and soil are piled on top of them. The increased pressure on the lower layers can cause metamorphism to happen. This is especially true when the rocks at the bottom are also affected by the heat from the magma below them.

Pressure also causes metamorphism at plate boundaries. Those are the places where the tectonic plates that make up Earth's crust meet. This type of metamorphism is called regional metamorphism. It happens when two tectonic plates push toward each other. Regional metamorphosis can occur over a very large area—hundreds or thousands of square miles.

As two tectonic plates collide, the edge of one plate usually sinks under the edge of the other plate. This is called subduction. When this happens, the rocks in the sinking plate edge are squeezed and **compacted** as they are pushed into the mantle. This pressure causes some of the rocks to change into metamorphic rocks.

TECTONIC PLATE SUBDUCTION

San Juan Mountains in Colorado

As the plate slides farther into the mantle, some rocks melt and become molten rock. The molten rock then pushes up into the solid rocks of the crust, which can cause even more metamorphic rocks to form. This creates mountain ranges and mountain belts. A range is a grouping of mountains, such as the Rocky Mountains in the western United States. A mountain belt is a grouping of mountain ranges. The Appalachian Belt in the eastern United States includes the White Mountains, Green Mountains, Catskills, and Blue Ridge Mountains.

The force of the plate collision also results in great pressure that creates cracks in Earth's crust called **faults**. In addition, moving plates cause friction along faults. The friction creates heat that can cause metamorphic changes in the rock.

compacted—pressed together
fault—a break in the rock of Earth's crust

CHAPTER 3
TYPES OF METAMORPHIC ROCK

There are many types of metamorphic rock. The type of metamorphic rock that forms is determined by two factors. The first factor is whether the metamorphosis is caused by heat, pressure, or both. The second factor is what kind of rock exists at the start of the process—the parent rock.

METAMORPHIC GRADES

Metamorphic rocks form over a range of temperatures and pressures. To help categorize the rocks, geologists assign "grades" to the rocks. The grades describe the conditions under which the rocks formed. The metamorphic grades are low, intermediate, and high.

Low-grade refers to rocks created by low pressures and temperatures just above 392°F (200°C). Slate and phyllite are low-grade metamorphic rocks. High-grade rocks form from very high pressures and temperatures from 1,472°F (800°C) to just below melting. Gneiss is a high-grade metamorphic rock. Intermediate-grade metamorphosis rocks form at pressures and temperatures between those of low- and high-grade rocks. Schist is an example of an intermediate-grade metamorphic rock.

METAMORPHIC GRADES

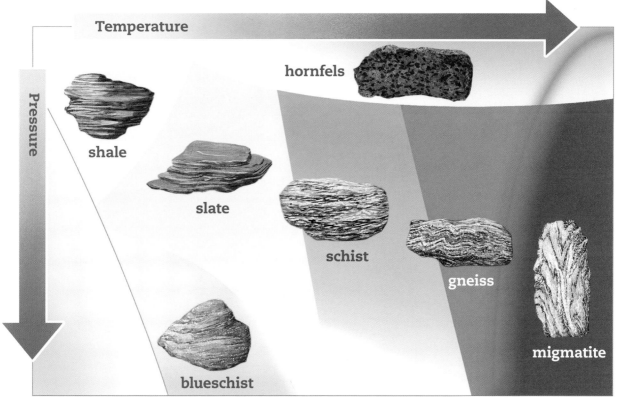

Temperature

Pressure

hornfels

shale

slate

schist

gneiss

migmatite

blueschist

FACT

Geologists look for certain minerals to find out how a metamorphic rock formed. They call these minerals "index minerals."

Shale is a sedimentary rock. It is a good example of a rock that can develop into different types of metamorphic rocks. Shale can become the metamorphic rocks slate, phyllite, schist, and gneiss. It just depends on how much heat and pressure are involved.

Slate can only be made from shale. Shale turns into slate through low-grade metamorphosis. Slate is a fine-grained metamorphic rock that is dark gray or black in color. Slate splits easily into thin, flat sheets. The word *slate* was commonly used in classrooms during the early 1900s. At that time, students would each have their own "slates" and write on them with chalk. These little chalkboards made out of pieces of the metamorphic rock slate were the perfect size for students to use in school. These mini chalkboards were used instead of paper because paper was rare and expensive.

Phyllite is what slate becomes under more heat and pressure. It is **foliated**, which means the minerals form layers and look like bands. Phyllite is often shiny because it includes the mineral mica.

phyllite

Schist and phyllite rocks are found in the Urenga mountain ridge in Russia.

foliated—composed of or capable of being separated into layers

Schist can be made from shale, but it can also be made from mudstone. Schist occurs through medium-grade metamorphosis. Schist is very different from slate, even though it can come from the same type of rock. Schist does not break into thin, flat sheets like slate does. Schist comes in many different colors, including green, gray, dark brown, silver, pink, and black. Schist is a medium-grained rock. That means that it has larger crystals than slate does.

Waves crash on schist rocks along Castelejo Beach in Portugal.

Gneiss is another metamorphic rock that can be made from shale, as well as from other rocks. Gneiss is formed under extremely high temperatures and pressures. That makes it a high-grade metamorphic rock. Gneiss has larger crystals than slate or schist, which means gneiss has a coarse-grained texture. Gneiss is also characterized by bands of minerals that are often bent and folded into interesting patterns. Gneiss usually comes in pink or gray colors.

Marble is a metamorphic rock formed out of the sedimentary rock limestone. Limestone is mostly made out of calcite, which is a form of calcium. Limestone is formed on the ocean floor out of seashells over millions of years. When limestone is heated to high temperatures, it turns into marble. Limestone is a rather soft rock, but marble is very hard. Marble is usually pure white, but it can also come in green, black, red, blue, and yellow. Marble can have beautiful patterns as well.

white marble

CHAPTER 4

LIFE SPAN OF METAMORPHIC ROCKS

Metamorphic rocks generally last a very long time. The hardness of the rocks and the minerals that make up the rocks make them long-lasting. Scientists believe that a metamorphic rock such as gneiss will last for millions of years. But some metamorphic rocks are even billions of years old. That does not mean the rocks will last forever. Eventually, they will continue in the rock cycle and turn into sedimentary rocks, igneous rocks, or another type of metamorphic rock.

Gneiss sedimentary rock formations on the southwestern coast of Western Australia.

Movements of Earth's tectonic plates drive the rock cycle. There are eight main large plates. As the plates move around, they slide and collide with one another. Geologists call these motions plate tectonics. These conditions produce certain kinds of igneous, sedimentary, and metamorphic rocks. The rocks are unique to each set of plate conditions. Plate tectonics allows geologists to figure out what Earth was like millions of years ago.

EARTH'S TECTONIC PLATES

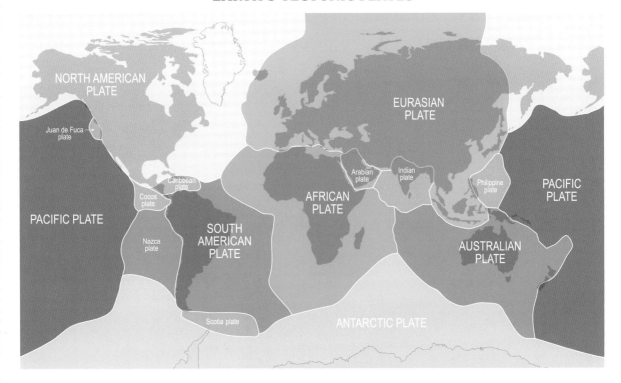

The moving together or pulling apart of tectonic plates allows molten rock in the mantle to form igneous rock. Magma rises to the surface through the **volcanic vents** and cools to form igneous rock that makes new crust. Such vents are usually in the ocean floor. Magma continues to melt the cooler rock around it as it rises higher and higher through the crust. As the magma burns through existing rock in the plate, it creates volcanoes.

Rising magma can form huge underground pools called **batholiths**. Magma can rise to the surface through a pipelike vent in a volcano and erupt as lava. The heat from magma underground in a batholith or volcanic vent can bake the existing rock and change it into metamorphic rock. Lava flowing onto the surface can also heat the rock on the ground and change it into metamorphic rock.

Parts of California's Yosemite National Park are found in the Sierra Nevada batholith.

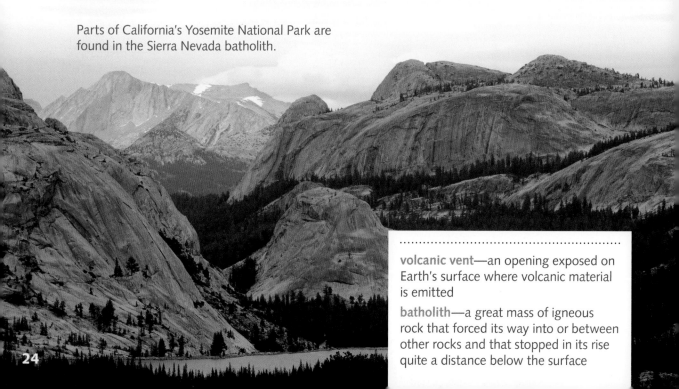

volcanic vent—an opening exposed on Earth's surface where volcanic material is emitted

batholith—a great mass of igneous rock that forced its way into or between other rocks and that stopped in its rise quite a distance below the surface

BLACK SMOKERS

Far below the ocean surface, there is a world where inky, black "clouds" boil out of vents, or cracks, in the seafloor. These clouds are fountains of hot water that carry chemicals up from rocks far below. Magma heats water that has seeped down through the rocks. Like water filtering through coffee grounds, the hot water dissolves minerals out of the rocks. The minerals contain sulfur, a chemical that created the black color. New rock forms from minerals in the water and builds up around the vents to form tall "chimneys."

This process is called hydrothermal metamorphism. It changes basalt, the igneous rock commonly found on the seafloor, into soapstone and serpentine. The hot water also deposits metals, such as gold and copper.

Strange forms of life, such as tubeworms and mussels, also exist around black smokers. There is no light that deep in the ocean. That means there are no plants, which depend on energy from the sun. Instead, the tubeworms and mussels eat bacteria that survive on the sulfur coming out of the deep-sea vents.

black smoker vent

Metamorphic rocks can be worn down before they become another type of rock. Like all rocks, metamorphic rocks are exposed to weathering and erosion. Wind, water, and other forces can slowly wear down and move the rock. Metamorphic rock can be weathered to form particles of sediment that become sedimentary rock. In this way, the rock cycle continues. The sedimentary rock that has formed from weathered metamorphic rock melts in the mantle and then hardens into igneous rock. The rock cycle begins anew.

weathering—breaking down of solid rock into smaller and smaller pieces by wind, water, glaciers, or plant roots

erosion—wearing away of rock or soil by wind, water, or ice

The materials in a metamorphic rock can also determine the rock's life span. For example, marble is a metamorphic rock made out of calcite, which is highly reactive to acids. If acid is poured on marble, the calcite will dissolve. Marble buildings and marble statues can be harmed by acid rain, which is caused by pollution. The acid rain will eat away marble buildings, sculptures, and rocks in nature until the stone crumbles and breaks into pieces.

Waves splash over metamorphic rocks on a rocky coast in Sri Lanka, Asia.

CHAPTER 5

USES FOR METAMORPHIC ROCKS

Metamorphic rocks are not as common as sedimentary and igneous rocks. Therefore, they are not used very often as building materials. When they are used, however, they have many purposes. Schist and gneiss, for example, are two metamorphic rocks that are great for buildings. Most important, they are hard rocks. They often have colorful and sparkly crystals, swirls, and layered bands in them. Schist and gneiss can also be crushed into small rocks for use in gravel and concrete.

Slate is another type of metamorphic rock used in construction. When split into flat sheets, it can be used as tiles for roofs and floors. Slate is a great rock for this purpose. It can be made into very thin pieces, and it is also waterproof.

Marble is another important building material. The ancient Greeks used it in their temples and sculptures. One example is the Parthenon, which was a temple to the goddess Athena. The Romans also used marble in their artwork. The most famous marble comes from a city in Italy named Carrara. As Michelangelo did, other sculptors and builders have used Carrara marble for centuries. Marble is still used today in artwork and in construction. Some people use marble as countertops and flooring for their kitchens and bathrooms.

FACT

Marble is used to make statues not only because it is strong and beautiful, but also because it is resistant to fire.

GLOSSARY

batholith (BATH-uh-lith)—a great mass of igneous rock that forced its way into or between other rocks and that stopped in its rise quite a distance below the surface

compacted (kuhm-PAKT-id)—pressed together

crystal (KRIS-tuhl)—a solid substance having a regular pattern of many flat surfaces

erosion (i-ROH-zhuhn)—wearing away of rock or soil by wind, water, or ice

fault (FAWLT)—a break in the rock of Earth's crust

foliated (FOH-lee-a-tid)—composed of or capable of being separated into layers

geologist (jee-AHL-uh-jist)—someone who studies minerals, rocks, and soil

hornfels (HORN-felz)—a metamorphic rock formed by the contact between mudstone or shale and a hot igneous body

melting point (MEL-ting POINT)—the temperature when a solid turns into a liquid when heated

tectonic plate (tek-TON-ik PLAYT)—a gigantic slab of Earth's crust that moves around on magma

volcanic vent (vol-KAN-ik VENT)—an opening exposed on Earth's surface where volcanic material is emitted

weathering (WETH-er-ing)—breaking down of solid rock into smaller and smaller pieces by wind, water, glaciers, or plant roots

READ MORE

Oxlade, Chris. *Minerals*. Rock On! Chicago: Heinemann Raintree, 2016.

Oxlade, Chris. *Rocks*. Rock On! Chicago: Heinemann Raintree, 2016.

Rajczak Nelson, Kristen. *What Are Metamorphic Rocks?* A Look at Earth's Rocks. New York: Gareth Stevens Publishing, 2018.

Spilsbury, Richard. *Metamorphic Rocks*. Earth's Rocky Past. New York: PowerKids Press, 2015.

INTERNET SITES

Use FactHound to find Internet sites related to this book.

Visit *www.facthound.com*

Just type in 9781543527025 and go.

 Check out projects, games and lots more at
www.capstonekids.com

CRITICAL THINKING QUESTIONS

1. What type of rocks can turn into metamorphic rock?

2. How is the type of metamorphic rock determined?

3. What types of metamorphic rocks can shale turn into?

INDEX